EXCELLENCE

Run with the Horses

6 STUDIES FOR INDIVIDUALS OR GROUPS

LifeGuide®
BIBLE STUDIES

EUGENE H. PETERSON

ivp

An imprint of InterVarsity Press
Downers Grove, Illinois

InterVarsity Press
P.O. Box 1400 | Downers Grove, IL 60515-1426
ivpress.com | email@ivpress.com

InterVarsity Press® is the publishing division of InterVarsity Christian Fellowship/USA®.
For information, visit intervarsity.org.

This study guide is based on and adapts material from *Run with the Horses* © 1983 by InterVarsity Christian
Fellowship of the United States of America.

The publisher cannot verify the accuracy or functionality of website URLs used in this book beyond the date
of publication.

Cover design: David Fassett

ISBN 978-1-5140-0602-3 (print) | ISBN 978-1-5140-0603-0 (digital)

Printed in the United States of America ♾

26 25 24 23 | 6 5 4 3 2 1

CONTENTS

GETTING THE MOST OUT OF *EXCELLENCE*

Why do so many people live so badly? Not so wickedly, but so inanely. Not so cruelly, but so stupidly. There is little to admire and less to imitate in the people who are prominent in our culture. We have celebrities but not saints.

This condition has produced an odd phenomenon: individuals who live trivial lives and then engage in evil acts in order to establish significance for themselves. Assassins, hijackers, and mass shooters attempt the gigantic leap from obscurity to fame by killing a prominent person or endangering the lives of numerous bystanders. Often they are successful. The mass media report their words and display their actions. Writers vie with one another in analyzing their motives and providing psychological profiles of them.

If, on the other hand, we look around for what it means to be a mature, whole, blessed person, we don't find much. These people are around, maybe as many of them as ever, but they aren't easy to pick out. No journalist interviews them. No talk show features them. They're not admired. They are not looked up to. They do not set trends. There is no cash value in them. No Oscars are given for integrity. At year's end no one compiles a list of the ten best-lived lives.

DULL VIRTUE?

In novels and poems and plays most of the memorable figures are either villains or victims. Good people, virtuous lives, mostly seem a bit dull. Jeremiah is a stunning exception. For most of my adult life he has attracted me. The complexity and intensity of his person caught and kept my attention. The captivating quality in the man is his goodness, his virtue, his excellence. He lived at his best. His was not a hothouse piety, for he lived through crushing storms of hostility and furies of bitter doubt. There is not a trace of smugness or complacency or naiveté in Jeremiah—every muscle in his body was stretched to the limits by fatigue, every thought in his mind subjected to rejection, every feeling in his heart put through fires of ridicule. Goodness in Jeremiah was not "being nice." It was something more like *prowess.*

There is a memorable passage concerning Jeremiah's life, when, worn down by the opposition and absorbed in self-pity, he was about to capitulate to an inner death. He was ready to abandon his unique calling in God and settle for being a Jerusalem statistic. At that critical moment he heard the reprimand:

> If you have raced with men on foot
>> and they have worn you out,
>> how can you compete with horses?
> If you stumble in safe country,
>> how will you manage in the thickets by the Jordan?
>> (Jeremiah 12:5)

Life is difficult, Jeremiah. Are you going to quit at the first wave of opposition? Are you going to retreat when you find that there is more to life than getting three meals a day and a dry place to sleep at night? Are you going to run home the minute you find that the mass of men and women are more interested in keeping their feet warm than in living at risk to the glory of God? Are you going to live cautiously or courageously? I called you to live at your best, to pursue righteousness, to sustain a drive toward excellence.

It is easier to relax in the embracing arms of The Average. Easier, but not better. Easier, but not more significant. Easier, but not more fulfilling. I called you to a life of purpose far beyond what you think yourself capable of living, and I promised you adequate strength to fulfill your destiny. Now at the first sign of difficulty you are ready to quit. If you are fatigued by this run-of-the-mill crowd of apathetic mediocrities, what will you do when the real race starts, the race with the swift and determined horses of excellence? What is it you really want, Jeremiah? Do you want to shuffle along with this crowd or to run with the horses?

It is unlikely, I think, that Jeremiah was spontaneous or quick in his reply to God's question. The ecstatic ideals for a new life had been splattered with the world's cynicism. The euphoric impetus of youthful enthusiasm no longer carried him. He weighed the options. He counted the cost. He tossed and turned in hesitation. The response when it came was not verbal but biographical. His life became his answer: "I'll run with the horses."

SUGGESTIONS FOR INDIVIDUAL STUDY

1. As you begin each study, pray that God will speak to you through his Word.

2. Read the introduction to the study and respond to the personal reflection question or exercise. This is designed to help you focus on God and on the theme of the study.

3. Each study deals with a particular passage—so that you can delve into the author's meaning in that context. Read and reread the passage to be studied. The questions are written using the language of the New International Version, so you may wish to use that version of the Bible. The New Revised Standard Version is also recommended.

4. This is an inductive Bible study, designed to help you discover for yourself what Scripture is saying. The study includes three types of questions. *Observation* questions ask about the basic facts: who, what, when, where, and how. *Interpretation* questions delve into the meaning of the passage. *Application* questions help you discover the implications of the text for growing in Christ. These three keys unlock the treasures of Scripture.

Write your answers to the questions in the spaces provided or in a personal journal. Writing can bring clarity and deeper understanding of yourself and of God's Word.

5. It might be good to have a Bible dictionary handy. Use it to look up any unfamiliar words, names, or places.

6. Use the prayer suggestion to guide you in thanking God for what you have learned and to pray about the applications that have come to mind.

7. You may want to go on to the suggestion under "Now or Later," or you may want to use that idea for your next study.

SUGGESTIONS FOR MEMBERS OF A GROUP STUDY

1. Come to the study prepared. Follow the suggestions for individual study mentioned above. You will find that careful preparation will greatly enrich your time spent in group discussion.

2. Be willing to participate in the discussion. The leader of your group will not be lecturing. Instead, he or she will be encouraging the members of the group to discuss what they have learned. The leader will be asking the questions that are found in this guide.

3. Stick to the topic being discussed. Your answers should be based on the verses which are the focus of the discussion and not on outside authorities such as commentaries or speakers. These studies focus on a particular passage of Scripture. Only rarely should you refer to other portions of the Bible. This allows for everyone to participate in in-depth study on equal ground.

4. Be sensitive to the other members of the group. Listen attentively when they describe what they have learned. You may be surprised by their insights! Each question assumes a variety of answers. Many questions do not have "right" answers, particularly questions that aim at meaning or application. Instead the questions push us to explore the passage more thoroughly.

When possible, link what you say to the comments of others. Also, be affirming whenever you can. This will encourage some of the more hesitant members of the group to participate.

5. Be careful not to dominate the discussion. We are sometimes so eager to express our thoughts that we leave too little opportunity for others to respond. By all means participate! But allow others to also.

6. Expect God to teach you through the passage being discussed and through the other members of the group. Pray that you will have an enjoyable and profitable time together, but also that as a result of the study you will find ways that you can take action individually and/or as a group.

7. Remember that anything said in the group is considered confidential and should not be discussed outside the group unless specific permission is given to do so.

8. If you are the group leader, you will find additional suggestions at the back of the guide.

ONE

PLEADING INADEQUACY

Jeremiah 1:4-19

If we are asked to do something that we know we cannot do, it is foolish to accept the assignment, for it soon becomes an embarrassment to everyone. God asked Jeremiah to do something he couldn't do. Naturally, he refused. The job Jeremiah refused was to be a prophet.

No job is more important, for what is more important than a persuasive presentation of the invisible but living reality—God? And what is more important than a convincing demonstration of the eternal meaning of the visible, ordinary stuff of daily life? But more important or not, Jeremiah refused. He was not qualified. He had not done well in the God courses in school. And he hadn't been around long enough to know how the world works. "'Alas, Sovereign LORD,' I said, 'I do not know how to speak; I am too young'" (Jeremiah 1:6).

There is an enormous gap between what we think we can do and what God calls us to do. Our ideas of what we can do or want to do are trivial; God's ideas for us are grand. God's call to Jeremiah to be a prophet parallels his call to us to be a person. The excuses we make are plausible; often they are statements of fact. But they are excuses all the same and are disallowed by our Lord, who says: "Do not say, 'I am too young.' You must go to everyone I send you to and say whatever I command you. Do not be afraid of them, for I am with you and will rescue you" (Jeremiah 1:7-8).

Group Discussion. Describe a time when someone asked you to do something you thought was over your head. What feelings did you have about attempting the task? What reasons did you have to not try? What did you do?

Personal Reflection. What helps you feel encouraged when you have a difficult task set before you?

The book of Jeremiah begins with the story of the prophet's call and how he responded. This passage introduces us to Jeremiah's character and sets up several key themes of the book. *Read Jeremiah 1:4-19.*

| **1.** Summarize God's calling to Jeremiah in this chapter.

| **2.** What is Jeremiah's initial reaction to God's call on his life (v. 6)?

3. How does God reassure Jeremiah that he is capable of being God's prophet?

4. What do you think would be challenging for Jeremiah in his prophetic role? What would be fulfilling?

5. Jeremiah was appointed by God to be a prophet to the nations (v. 5). God has a unique and original adventure for each of us. What has God appointed you to do or to be?

6. We too are good at pleading inadequacy in order to avoid living at the best God calls us to. What reasons have you used to resist God's call on your life?

7. God showed Jeremiah two visions in this dialogue (vv. 11-16). What is the significance of the vision in verses 11-12?

What is the significance of the vision in verses 13-16?

8. In verse 19 the Lord says, "They will fight against you but will not overcome you, for I am with you and will rescue you." In what ways has God communicated reassurance that he will help you to become the person you are called to be—even in the face of opposition?

9. Jeremiah lived in a changing and dangerous world, much like our own. How do you see God's hand controlling evil in the world?

10. How can you be more open to both God's call and God's reassurance to you?

 Offer God your praise for his work in your life—in the past, present, and future.

NOW OR LATER

Make a list of people, experiences, Scripture passages, or symbols that remind you of God's presence in your life. Each day focus on one item on the list, thanking God for it.

TWO

IMAGE VERSUS SUBSTANCE

Jeremiah 7:1-15

Words are important—immensely important. What we say and the way we say it expresses what is most personal and intimate in us. But mindlessly repeating holy words no more creates a relationship than saying "I love you" twenty times a day makes us skilled lovers.

The outside is a lot easier to reform than the inside. Going to the right church and saying the right words is a lot easier than working out a life of justice and love among the people you work and live with. Showing up at church once a week and saying a hearty amen is a lot easier than engaging in a life of daily prayer and Scripture meditation, which develops into concern for poverty and injustice, hunger and war.

Are the people who do this deliberately trying to pull the wool over the eyes of their neighbors and fake God into blessing them? Some are, but for most I don't think so. I don't think they are trying to get by with anything. I think they have lived for so long on the basis of outward appearances that they have no feel for inward reality. We live in a culture where a new beginning is far more attractive than a long follow-through. Images are important. Beginnings are important. But an image without substance is a lie. A beginning without a continuation is a lie. This is the important message Jeremiah has for Israel.

Group Discussion. How does our culture emphasize image over substance? (Consider movies, TV shows, music, and politics.)

Personal Reflection. How do you think people perceive you? When has someone's perception of you influenced your actions?

After decades of widespread idolatry and wickedness under the kings Manasseh and Amon, King Josiah brought reform to Judah. Jeremiah participated in this reform with his preaching. But when the prophet watched the people worshiping at the temple, he had some hard words about the depth of change they had really embraced. *Read Jeremiah 7:1-15.*

| **1.** Describe the attitude of the Israelites as they approached worship.

| **2.** What deceptive words were the Israelites trusting in?

3. Why were these words appealing?

4. In what ways might your church or fellowship cling to deceptive words?

5. In what ways did the Israelites need to change (vv. 5-8)?

6. What is the connection between worship and how we live our lives?

7. How has worship affected the way you live?

8. What are the consequences of obeying or disobeying God according to these verses (vv. 3, 7, 14-15)?

9. False prophets were deceiving the Israelites and keeping them from listening to God: "I spoke to you again and again, but you did not listen" (v. 13). What keeps you from hearing God?

10. How does living in a society that emphasizes outward appearances affect our ability to be honest with ourselves?

11. How do deceptive words (image) keep you from experiencing and responding to God in true worship (substance)?

 Thank God for the privilege that he extends to us of belonging to him and coming before him in worship.

NOW OR LATER

To prepare for corporate worship this week, ask God how you need to change your ways and actions (v. 5). Spend time in confession and listen for God's word of forgiveness and restoration.

THREE

GOD'S SHAPING HAND

Jeremiah 18:1-18

T**ry to imagine how** life would change if we had no containers in which to store anything: no pots and pans, no bowls and dishes, no cans and barrels, no cardboard boxes and paper bags, no grain silos and oil storage tanks. Life would be reduced to what we could manage in a single day with what we could hold in our hands at one time. Pottery made it possible for communities to develop. Life was extended beyond the immediate, beyond the urgent.

There is something else that is just as important. No one has ever been able to make a clay pot that is just a clay pot. Every pot is also an art form. Pottery is always changing its shape as potters find new proportions, different ways to shape the pots in pleasing combinations of curves. There is no pottery that besides being useful does not also show evidence of beauty. Pottery is artistically shaped, designed, painted, glazed, fired. It is one of the most functional items in life; it is also one of the most beautiful.

We commonly separate the useful and the beautiful, the necessary and the elegant. We build featureless office buildings and ugly factories for our necessary work; then we build museums to contain the objects of beauty.

Each human being is an inseparable union of necessity and freedom. There is no human being who is not useful with a part to play in what God is doing. And there is no human being who is not unique with special lines and colors and forms distinct from anyone else.

All this became clear to Jeremiah in the potter's house: the brute fact of the clay, lumpish and inert, shaped for a purpose by the hands of the potter, and then, as it took shape, the realization of the uniquely designed individuality and wide-ranging usefulness it would acquire as a finished pot. God shapes us for his eternal purposes, and he begins right here. The dust out of which we are made and the image of God into which we are made are one and the same.

Group Discussion. Think of a time when you had a plan to do something but you couldn't complete the project because you needed someone else who wasn't willing to help. What were your reactions, internal and external, to the other person?

Personal Reflection. When has a person who seemed ordinary on the outside influenced you in a way that was particularly meaningful?

In seventh-century Israel the potter's house was a fixture in every community. Everyone knew the potter's work was necessary for the maintenance of everyday life. God sent Jeremiah to observe this ordinary activity of shaping clay, and Jeremiah's imagination went to work as he stood watching. *Read Jeremiah 18:1-18.*

1. What words would you use to describe God's feelings about the nation of Israel in this passage?

2. What do you think Jeremiah might be feeling?

3. What would be a contemporary parallel to the analogy of the potter: someone who tries to create something but needs the participation of whatever is being molded?

4. In what ways did the nation of Israel resist being molded by God (vv. 13-15)?

5. What was God's response to their resistance (vv. 16-17)?

6. How would you summarize God's plea to his people in this passage?

7. What are some of the ways that people today resist being molded by God?

8. Jeremiah had to pay a price for allowing God to mold him. In fact he was repeatedly criticized, cursed, slandered, and thrown into jail (v. 18). What price have you had to pay for following God?

9. When has God showed patience with you, starting over in his effort to mold you?

10. Knowing that we all sometimes resist God's workings, why do you think God keeps working with us?

11. What are some actions—however small—you can take to cooperate with God's molding you into a more mature Christian?

12. What are some possible frustrations or hardships you might face by allowing God to mold you?

 Talk to God about the work he is doing and will be doing in you. Freely express your fear and hesitation as well as your excitement.

NOW OR LATER

Meditate on the image of God as a potter shaping you or your community. How are you responding to his work? You may also want to look up the similar uses of this metaphor in Isaiah 29, 45, and 64.

HONESTY

Jeremiah 15:10-21

In the spring of 1980, Rosie Ruiz was the first woman to cross the finish line of the Boston Marathon. She had the laurel wreath placed on her head in a blaze of lights and cheering. She was completely unknown in the world of running. An incredible feat! Her first race a victory in the prestigious Boston Marathon!

But then questions were asked. No one had seen her along the 26.2 mile course. The truth came out: she had jumped into the race during the last mile. There was immediate and widespread interest in Rosie. Why would she do that when it was certain that she would be found out? Athletic performance cannot be faked. But she never admitted her fraud. She repeatedly said that she would run another marathon to validate her ability. Somehow she never did.

One interviewer concluded that she really believed she had run the complete Boston Marathon and won. She was analyzed as a sociopath. She lied convincingly and naturally with no sense of conscience, no sense of reality in terms of right and wrong, acceptable and unacceptable behavior. She appeared healthy and intelligent. But there was no moral sense to give coherence to her social actions.

In reading about Rosie I thought of all the people I know who want to get in on the finish but who cleverly arrange not to run the race. They appear in church on Sunday wreathed in smiles, entering into the celebration, but there is no personal life that leads up to it or out from it. Occasionally they engage in spectacular acts of love and compassion in public. They are plausible and convincing. But in the end they do not run the race, believing through the tough times, praying through the lonely, angry, hurt hours. They have no sense for what is *real* in religion. The proper label for such a person is *religiopath*.

No one becomes human the way Jeremiah was human by posing in a posture of victory. It was his prayers, hidden but persistent, that brought him to the human wholeness and spiritual sensitivity that we want to emulate. What we do in secret determines the soundness of who we are in public.

Group Discussion. Recall a time when you felt deserted by God. What were the circumstances that helped you to feel God's presence again?

Personal Reflection. Think of the most memorable prayer experiences you have had. What did they all have in common?

In seven passages in the book of Jeremiah, the prophet speaks in the first person. Jeremiah's inner life is revealed in these confessions. When he was out of the public eye he was passionate with God—he prayed. The confession in Jeremiah 15 is one example. *Read Jeremiah 15:10-21.*

1. What does this passage tell you about the kind of person Jeremiah is?

2. What are Jeremiah's concerns in his prayer?

3. Think of a time when you felt similar to Jeremiah. What did you do with those feelings?

4. Jeremiah was extremely honest in his prayer to God. When do you find it difficult to be honest with God?

5. What do you think Jeremiah wants God to tell him?

6. What is God's response to Jeremiah's heartfelt prayer (vv. 19-21)?

7. Think of a time when God's response to your prayer was un-
expected or surprising to you. What were the circumstances?

8. Jeremiah, God's prophet, found himself alone in following God's commands to live a holy life. Why do you think God called Jeremiah to repentance in verse 19?

9. Most Christians go through periods when what God asks of them seems unreasonable or unfair. How do you think we can respond well in such times?

10. What does your prayer life reveal about you?

11. How can you be more honest with God, and yourself, when you pray?

 Begin the conversation with God by expressing the concerns that are on your mind today—even if they seem trivial or unreasonable. Be sure to allow time to listen for God's response.

NOW OR LATER

Jeremiah must have been open to whatever God's response would be. This week, make it your goal to pray honestly and then seek to hear God's response to your prayers, not just what you want to hear.

FIVE

OBEDIENCE

Jeremiah 35

The moral level of our society is shameful. The spiritual integrity of our culture is an embarrassment. Any part of our lives that is turned over to the crowd makes it and us worse. The larger the crowd, the smaller our lives. Pliny the Elder once said that the Romans, when they couldn't make a building beautiful, made it big. The practice continues to be popular: if we can't do it well, we make it larger. We add dollars to our incomes, rooms to our houses, activities to our schedules, appointments to our calendars. And the quality of our lives diminishes with each addition.

On the other hand, every time that we retrieve a part of our lives from the crowd and respond to God's call to us, we are that much more ourselves, more human. Every time we reject the habits of the crowd and practice the disciplines of faith, we become a little more alive. In this passage Jeremiah shows what obedience looks like when a group of people make a commitment to hear God's call.

Group Discussion. Think of an individual or group that stands out from the crowd because they live by their own standards. What are their attractive qualities?

Personal Reflection. What keeps you from rejecting the habits of people around you and living by different standards?

The majority of people in Jerusalem may have understood and admired the way Jeremiah lived, but they did not join him in his spiritual intensity. They were conditioned to follow the crowd. The Recabites, a group of metalworkers who roamed the country and lived in tents, stood out from everyone else. *Read Jeremiah 35.*

1. What was unique about the Recabites (vv. 6-7)?

2. What did God tell Jeremiah to offer the Recabites?

3. What was the context of this offer?

4. What does their refusal tell you about the Recabites?

5. What parallel does Jeremiah draw between the standards of the Recabites and what God expected from the people of Jerusalem (vv. 12-16)?

6. How had the people responded to God's messages through the prophets?

7. In what areas of your life do you sense God calling you to higher standards than the people or patterns around you?

8. What factors might have made it easier for the Recabites to keep the commands of their ancestors?

9. What factors can you include in your life to help you remain faithful to God's calling for you?

10. In verse 19 God makes a promise to the Recabites, based on their obedience, that they will always be allowed to serve him. How have you seen God give you opportunities to serve when you have been faithful to God's standards?

11. List choices you make that fit in with society around you. Do any of these choices keep you from living up to God's standards? How?

Pray that God will give you the courage and conviction to overcome the factors in your life that keep you from following him.

NOW OR LATER

Consider a person or group you thought of in the group discussion for this session. Try to read more about them or have a conversation with them if possible, and reflect on how they stand out from the crowd. How does their example give you inspiration or insight?

SIX

MAKING THE BEST OF IT

Jeremiah 29:1-14

O ften we find ourselves in places we don't want to be with people we don't want to be with. We face decisions on how we will respond to these "exile" conditions. We can say: "I don't like it; I want to be where I was ten years ago. How can you expect me to throw myself into what I don't like—that would be sheer hypocrisy. What sense is there in taking risks and tiring myself out among people I don't even like in a place where I have no future?"

Or we can say: "I will do my best with what is here. Far more important than the climate of this place, the economics of this place, the neighbors in this place, is the God of this place. God is here with me. What I am experiencing right now is on ground that was created by him and with people whom he loves. It's just as possible to live out the will of God here as any place else. Change is hard. Building relationships in unfamiliar and hostile surroundings is difficult. But if that is what it means to be alive and human, I will do it."

Will we live on the basis of what we don't have or what we do have? This was Jeremiah's choice.

Group Discussion. What issues in your life seem to use up your energy or distract your attention?

Personal Reflection. Most of us have a vision for how we think our lives should be arranged so that God can use us most effectively. What does your vision look like?

Most of the people of Judah were taken into exile in 587 BC. They were uprooted from the place in which they were born and forced to travel seven hundred miles to Babylon. The reason for exile was clear: Jeremiah and other prophets had preached the need for faithfulness to God, but the nation had rejected this message. Jeremiah was left behind in the land of Judah (Jeremiah 40:1-6). Yet he received a prophetic word for his people in Babylon, which he sent by letter. *Read Jeremiah 29:1-14.*

1. What is the situation Jeremiah sent his letter into?

2. What were some of the changes the exiles had to learn to deal with?

3. What is the essence of Jeremiah's instructions in verses 4-9?

4. Why do you think Jeremiah found it necessary to give this message?

5. Think of a time when you felt like an exile in a strange place. What emotions did you experience?

6. How did your relationship with God change during that time?

7. Reread verses 10-14. What possible reactions would you expect from the exiles in Babylon when they heard these words?

8. What can the exiles hope for? What is the basis for these hopes?

9. What parallels do you see between the Jews who were exiled and your life as a Christian?

10. How have you seen God at work in your life even when things didn't turn out the way you expected?

11. How do the words of verses 10-14 encourage you as you try to remain faithful to God in a strange and change-filled society?

Ask God to show you the gifts he offers you in the midst of the physical place and time you are dwelling in. Thank him for the good gifts you find in culture.

NOW OR LATER

Think of three ways that you can be more open to being used by God in the situation you find yourself in. What next steps can you take?

LEADER'S NOTES

My grace is sufficient for you.

2 CORINTHIANS 12:9

L eading a Bible discussion can be an enjoyable and rewarding experience. But it can also be *scary*—especially if you've never done it before. If this is your feeling, you're in good company. When God asked Moses to lead the Israelites out of Egypt, he replied, "Lord. Please send someone else" (Exodus 4:13). It was the same with Solomon, Jeremiah, and Timothy, but God helped these people in spite of their weaknesses, and he will help you as well.

You don't need to be an expert on the Bible or a trained teacher to lead a Bible discussion. The idea behind these inductive studies is that the leader guides group members to discover for themselves what the Bible has to say. This method of learning will allow group members to remember much more of what is said than a lecture would.

These studies are designed to be led easily. As a matter of fact, the flow of questions through the passage from observation to interpretation to application is so natural that you may feel that the studies lead themselves. This study guide is also flexible. You can use it with a variety of groups—student, professional, neighborhood, or church groups. Each study takes forty-five to sixty minutes in a group setting.

There are some important facts to know about group dynamics and encouraging discussion. The suggestions listed below should enable you to effectively and enjoyably fulfill your role as leader.

PREPARING FOR THE STUDY

1. Ask God to help you understand and apply the passage in your own life. Unless this happens, you will not be prepared to lead others. Pray too for the various members of the group. Ask God to open your hearts to the message of his Word and motivate you to action.

2. Read the introduction to the entire guide to get an overview of the entire book and the issues which will be explored.

3. As you begin each study, read and reread the assigned Bible passage to familiarize yourself with it.

4. This study guide is based on the New International Version of the Bible. It will help you and the group if you use this translation as the basis for your study and discussion.

5. Carefully work through each question in the study. Spend time in meditation and reflection as you consider how to respond.

6. Write your thoughts and responses in the space provided in the study guide. This will help you to express your understanding of the passage clearly.

7. It might help to have a Bible dictionary handy. Use it to look up any unfamiliar words, names, or places. (For additional help on how to study a passage, see chapter five of *How to Lead a LifeGuide Bible Study,* InterVarsity Press.)

8. Consider how you can apply the Scripture to your life. Remember that the group will follow your lead in responding to the studies. They will not go any deeper than you do.

9. Once you have finished your own study of the passage, familiarize yourself with the leader's notes for the study you are leading. These are designed to help you in several ways. First, they tell you the purpose the study guide author had in mind when writing the study. Take time to think through how the study questions work together to accomplish that purpose. Second, the notes provide you with additional background information or suggestions on group dynamics for various questions. This information can be useful when people have difficulty understanding or answering a question. Third, the leader's notes can alert you to potential problems you may encounter during the study.

10. If you wish to remind yourself of anything mentioned in the leader's notes, make a note to yourself below that question in the study.

LEADING THE STUDY

1. Begin the study on time. Open with prayer, asking God to help the group to understand and apply the passage.

2. Be sure that everyone in your group has a study guide. Encourage the group to prepare beforehand for each discussion by reading the introduction to the guide and by working through the questions in the study.

3. At the beginning of your first time together, explain that these studies are meant to be discussions, not lectures. Encourage the members of the group to participate. However, do not put pressure on those who may be hesitant to speak during the first few sessions. You may want to suggest the following guidelines to your group.

- Stick to the topic being discussed.
- Your responses should be based on the verses which are the focus of the discussion and not on outside authorities such as commentaries or speakers.
- These studies focus on a particular passage of Scripture. Only rarely should you refer to other portions of the Bible. This allows for everyone to participate in in-depth study on equal ground.
- Anything said in the group is considered confidential and will not be discussed outside the group unless specific permission is given to do so.
- We will listen attentively to each other and provide time for each person present to talk.
- We will pray for each other.

4. Have a group member read the introduction at the beginning of the discussion.

5. Every session begins with a group discussion question. The question or activity is meant to be used before the passage is read. The question introduces the theme of the study and encourages group members to begin to open up. Encourage as many members as possible to participate, and be ready to get the discussion going with your own response.

This section is designed to reveal where our thoughts or feelings need to be transformed by Scripture. That is why it is especially important not to read the passage before the discussion question is asked. The passage will tend to color the honest reactions people would otherwise give because they are, of course, supposed to think the way the Bible does.

You may want to supplement the group discussion question with an icebreaker to help people get comfortable. See the community section of InterVarsity Press's *Small Group Idea Book* for more ideas.

You also might want to use the personal reflection question with your group. Either allow a time of silence for people to respond individually or discuss it together.

6. Have a group member (or members if the passage is long) read aloud the passage to be studied. Then give people several minutes to read the passage again silently so that they can take it all in.

7. Question 1 will generally be an overview question designed to briefly survey the passage. Encourage the group to look at the whole passage, but try to avoid getting sidetracked by questions or issues that will be addressed later in the study.

8. As you ask the questions, keep in mind that they are designed to be used just as they are written. You may simply read them aloud. Or you may prefer to express them in your own words.

There may be times when it is appropriate to deviate from the study guide. For example, a question may have already been answered. If so, move on to the next question. Or someone may raise an important question not covered in the guide. Take time to discuss it, but try to keep the group from going off on tangents.

9. Avoid answering your own questions. If necessary, repeat or rephrase them until they are clearly understood. Or point out something you read in the leader's notes to clarify the context or meaning. An eager group quickly becomes passive and silent if they think the leader will do most of the talking.

10. Don't be afraid of silence. People may need time to think about the question before formulating their answers.

11. Don't be content with just one answer. Ask, "What do the rest of you think?" or "Anything else?" until several people have given answers to the question.

12. Acknowledge all contributions. Try to be affirming whenever possible. Never reject an answer. If it is clearly off base, ask, "Which verse led you to that conclusion?" or again, "What do the rest of you think?"

13. Don't expect every answer to be addressed to you, even though this will probably happen at first. As group members become more at ease, they will begin to truly interact with each other. This is one sign of healthy discussion.

14. Don't be afraid of controversy. It can be very stimulating. If you don't resolve an issue completely, don't be frustrated. Move on and keep it in mind for later. A subsequent study may solve the problem.

15. Periodically summarize what the group has said about the passage. This helps to draw together the various ideas mentioned and gives continuity to the study. But don't preach.

16. At the end of the Bible discussion, you may want to allow group members a time of quiet to work on an idea under "Now or Later." Then discuss what you experienced. Or you may want to encourage group members to work on these ideas between meetings. Give an opportunity during the session for people to talk about what they are learning.

17. Conclude your time together with conversational prayer, adapting the prayer suggestion at the end of the study to your group. Ask for God's help in following through on the commitments you've made.

18. End on time.

Many more suggestions and helps are found in *How to Lead a LifeGuide Bible Study,* which is part of the LifeGuide Bible Study series.

COMPONENTS OF SMALL GROUPS

A healthy small group should do more than study the Bible. There are four components to consider as you structure your time together.

Nurture. Small groups help us to grow in our knowledge and love of God. Bible study is the key to making this happen and is the foundation of your small group.

Community. Small groups are a great place to develop deep friendships with other Christians. Allow time for informal interaction before and after each study. Plan activities and games that will help you get to know each other. Spend time having fun together—going on a picnic or cooking dinner together.

Worship and prayer. Your study will be enhanced by spending time praising God together in prayer or song. Pray for each other's needs—and keep track of how God is answering prayer in your group. Ask God to help you to apply what you are learning in your study.

Outreach. Reaching out to others can be a practical way of applying what you are learning, and it will keep your group from becoming self-focused. Host a series of evangelistic discussions for your friends or neighbors. Clean up the yard of an elderly friend. Serve at a soup kitchen together, or spend a day working on a Habitat house.

Many more suggestions and helps in each of these areas are found in *Small Group Idea Book.* Information on building a small group can be found in *Small Group Leaders' Handbook* and *The Big Book on Small Groups* (both from InterVarsity Press). Reading through one of these books would be worth your time.

STUDY 1. PLEADING INADEQUACY. JEREMIAH 1:4-19.

PURPOSE: To explore God's call to each of us and how we can respond positively.

Question 3. God's reassurance to Jeremiah may not seem very comforting to us. God does not send us into the life of faith because we are qualified; he chooses us in order to qualify us for what he wants us to be and do. Yet God makes it clear to Jeremiah that if he lives up to his calling, God's presence will protect and sustain him.

Questions 5-6. While few of us are called by God in the same way as Jeremiah, God does have a mission for each of us to be a part of. And like Jeremiah most of us have more than enough excuses ready. We offer excuses because we are convinced that we are plain and ordinary. The town or city that we live in, the neighborhood we grew up in, the friends we are stuck with—all seem undramatic. We see no way to be significant in such settings. Yet something very different takes place in the life of faith: each person discovers all the elements of a unique and original adventure. God's creative genius is endless. Each life is a fresh canvas on which he uses lines and colors, shades and lights, textures and proportions that he has never used before. It is as we participate in what God initiates in our lives that we find purpose.

Question 7. Both of these visions may seem strange to us, but each communicated something deep and vital to Jeremiah. The almond tree is one of the earliest trees to bloom in Palestine. As a sign of spring, it is an anticipation, a promise of what is to come. There is also a word-play between the Hebrew words for *almond* and *watching*. God is promising Jeremiah that he will take care of Jeremiah and his message, and the almond branch becomes a visible reminder of that reassurance.

The boiling pot is partially explained in the passage. In the changing world order of Jeremiah's time the military threat was the Neo-Babylonian empire, which within a few years would attack Jerusalem. While this vision is negative, there are two implications that may have been comforting for Jeremiah: first, that the coming evil was under God's control, and second, that it did have limits.

Question 8. Jeremiah's assurances seemed to come from God directly; most people are not so fortunate. So encourage group members to think of people or events that God has used to speak to them. Often God's messages come through very subjective experiences. Other people may find reassuring signs in nature, like Jeremiah with the almond branch.

Question 9. This is not an easy question, and group members may be intimidated by it. Give them time to think, and be ready to jump in with your own example. Group members will feel more comfortable if you take the lead in showing them that they can be vulnerable.

STUDY 2. IMAGE VERSUS SUBSTANCE. JEREMIAH 7:1-15.

PURPOSE: To learn to recognize the difference between image and substance.

Question 1. Many of the Israelites evidently approached worship with a sense of complacency, stupidly pleased with themselves, putting their faith in the latest reform slogan.

Question 2. False prophets were leading the people to believe that God's presence in Jerusalem, and especially in the temple, meant that God's power would always protect those within the city. Carried to its extreme, this meant that their actions had no effect on God's promised protection, despite Jeremiah's persistent preaching to the contrary. "The threefold saying in verse 4 sounds like a mantra, as if it could protect the people from harm and destruction, but this is a false, deceptive concept. Worshiping God and serving him in the temple according to the rules can never be an excuse for ignoring his commandments in the rest of life" (Hetty Lalleman, *Jeremiah and Lamentations*, Tyndale Old Testament Commentaries [Downers Grove, IL: IVP Academic, 2013], 107).

Question 6. Our lives are defined by our worship—by what we choose to worship, by the intensity and depth of our worship. Meaning and the importance of values become clear when our worship has integrity. When it does not, then our lives become shapeless and confused.

STUDY 3. GOD'S SHAPING HAND. JEREMIAH 18:1-18.

PURPOSE: To understand how God wants to shape us and how we participate in that process.

Question 1. God's words to and through Jeremiah show a wide range of emotions. Although the most obvious emotions are negative, note the tenderness in God's willingness to change his plans if Israel repents. (Consider that in Jonah 3 God does indeed change his plan for the city of Nineveh.) God wanted to be merciful to Israel and, like the potter, try again to mold the people.

Question 2. If members of the group are uncomfortable hypothesizing about Jeremiah's feelings, ask them to put themselves in his sandals and express what their feelings would be.

Question 3. One example that might shed light on Jeremiah's analogy is the idea of a parent or teacher trying to mold a child into a mature person. This might help group members focus on the emotional investment God had in Israel.

Question 4. For a more detailed list see Jeremiah 7:1-11. In short, the people of Israel had not lived up to their end of the covenant with God.

The most obvious sign of this was their recurring worship of the false gods of their neighbors.

Question 7. Our resistance to God may not be as obvious as what Jeremiah denounced Israel for. However, many of us, even Christians, place goals, ideas, or values above God's desires for us. It might also be good to try to identify some of the underlying reasons that people resist God's working. For example, one reason the Israelites made idols was because they needed the reassurance of something concrete and physical, instead of trusting in an unseen God.

Question 8. Also see Jeremiah 20. Few people in Western nations will face anything like Jeremiah's struggles. However, even in places where Christianity is accepted, Christians face a choice between a religion that supports and reinforces cultural models of success and an encounter with the living God, which may require going against popular ideas, values, and choices. For those who choose the latter, anything (mockery, pain, renunciation, self-denial) will be accepted in order to deepen and extend the relationship with God.

STUDY 4. HONESTY. JEREMIAH 15:10-21.

PURPOSE: To discover how Jeremiah's life of prayer enabled him to be God's true servant.

Question 1. If there is confusion, it may be good to outline the dialogue of the passage. Verse 10 is Jeremiah speaking, rhetorically, to his mother. Verses 11-14 are God's response—Jeremiah will be delivered and his enemies defeated. Verses 15-18 are Jeremiah explicitly praying to God, and in 19-21 God responds again.

Question 2. Jeremiah is really feeling sorry for himself. He is scared, lonely, hurt, and angry. He feels that God's call on his life has robbed him of the comforts of being "normal." In the next chapter God will tell him not to marry and have children. He really feels as if he is an island. He was probably both attracted to the idea of being accepted by his fellow Israelites and repelled by their lifestyles. And deep down, he wanted to know that he was making a difference.

Question 5. Jeremiah is in some sense desperate. Desperate to hear that things will turn out all right, desperate to know that God cares about him, desperate to know that God is really in control. But he also wants to hear that things are going to get easier, not harder.

Question 6. Jeremiah's role in the prayer is to be honest with God and then to listen to God. God's role in the prayer is to restore and save Jeremiah. But he doesn't do it by giving easy answers. Instead, God feels Jeremiah's pain but does not indulge it. God calls Jeremiah to repent and reestablish God's priorities in his life. As a result, God promises to renew Jeremiah.

Question 8. Jeremiah needed to be reminded of what is important in life: loving his God and following his call. Jeremiah yearned, as we all do, for acceptance and an easier task; he had allowed the views of his neighbors to cloud his vision for what God had called him to do.

Question 9. Many of us are tempted, like Jeremiah surely was, to compare our commitment and perseverance with what our society shows as acceptable or normal. When we do we are tricked into false feelings about how good and honorable we are. Instead, we need to realize that as Christians we are measured in comparison to our Lord, who not only asks the impossible of us, but gives us grace and his presence in our task.

STUDY 5. OBEDIENCE. JEREMIAH 35.

PURPOSE: To explore what it means to follow God obediently, and to discover the help that we can find as we serve God in community.

Group Discussion. If the group has difficulty thinking of examples, you might mention the Amish or Mennonites, groups that refuse to adapt to many of the "conveniences" of modern life. Individuals who come to mind might include Mother Teresa or people who use their status or fame to advocate for issues of justice.

Question 1. The Recabites were, in a sense, defined by what set them apart from the rest of Israelite society. In a society that increasingly depended on the stability of a central government and its alliances, the Recabites must have seemed to be a people of uncommon simplicity and faith. We know very little about them. In fact, this passage is the only time they are mentioned in the Bible. Several theories exist to explain their lifestyle, including that they were throwbacks to a simpler, more religious form of Israel, or that they were in the military-defense business and needed mobility and a strong sense of unity. (See the discussion in Eugene H. Peterson, *Run with the Horses*, chapter 11.)

Questions 2-3. Not only does Jeremiah ask the Recabites to go against their vows, but he does so in the temple, in a public place, where they would have been seen by both God and other people.

Question 5. God's expectations for his people often seemed strange when compared to the surrounding nations, who worshiped various gods of nature. They also no doubt seemed arbitrary and silly to those who forgot the context of the covenant, just as the way of life of the Recabites must have seemed strange and unnecessary to those who didn't understand it.

Question 8. Regardless of why they followed their way of life, we can safely assume that the Recabites had several things going for them. They had a shared heritage, which gave them a strong sense of identity. They also appeared to have a strong sense of unity. And naturally it is often easier to live up to a standard when those around you are also trying to do so.

STUDY 6. MAKING THE BEST OF IT. JEREMIAH 29:1-14.

PURPOSE: To find courage to live as Christians in the midst of an ungodly culture.

Question 1. The basic scenario is seen in verses 1-3. However, more information can be inferred from later in the chapter. Three false prophets—Ahab, Zedekiah, and Shemaiah—told the people what they wanted to hear: "Hang on a little longer and we'll get back. It can't be much longer." They even claimed their words came from God (vv. 21-32).

Question 4. The exiles had listened to the lies of the false prophets. They wanted to believe that they would soon return to Jerusalem and everything would be okay again. Then they would have no need to develop relationships or care about Babylon at all. Jeremiah's letter was a reminder to them that God was not going to rescue them immediately and that they needed to get on with their lives.

Question 8. In this letter, God assures the people that they will prosper in Babylon, return to their land after seventy years, and have a renewed relationship with God. They can be confident in these hopes because of God's promise, plans, and desire to be in relationship with them (vv. 10-14).

Eugene H. Peterson (1932–2018) was a pastor, scholar, author, and poet. He wrote more than thirty books, including his widely acclaimed paraphrase of the Bible, The Message: The Bible in Contemporary Language; *his memoir,* The Pastor; *and the best-selling spiritual formation classic* A Long Obedience in the Same Direction.

WHAT SHOULD
WE STUDY NEXT?

LifeGuide®
BIBLE STUDIES

Since 1985 LifeGuide® Bible Studies have provided solid inductive Bible study content with field-tested questions that get groups talking—making for a one-of-a-kind Bible study experience. This series has more than 120 titles on Old and New Testament books, character studies, and topical studies. IVP's LifeGuide Finder is a great tool for searching for your next study topic: https://ivpress.com/lifeguidefinder.

Here are some ideas to get you started.

BIBLE BOOKS

An in-depth study of a Bible book is one of the richest experiences you could have in opening up the riches of Scripture. Many groups begin with a Gospel such as Mark or John. These guides are divided into two parts so that if twenty or twenty-six weeks feels like too much to do at once, the group can feel free to do half of the studies and take a break with another topic.

A shorter letter such as Philippians or Ephesians is also a great way to start. Shorter Old Testament studies include Ruth, Esther, and Job.

TOPICAL SERIES

Here are a few ideas of short series you might put together to cover a year of curriculum on a theme.

Christian Formation: *Christian Beliefs* (12 studies by Stephen D. Eyre), *Christian Character* (12 studies by Andrea Sterk & Peter Scazzero), *Christian Disciplines* (12 studies by Andrea Sterk & Peter Scazzero), *Evangelism* (12 studies by Rebecca Pippert & Ruth Siemens).

Building Community: *Christian Community* (10 studies by Rob Suggs), *Friendship* (10 studies by Carolyn Nystrom), *Spiritual Gifts* (8 studies by R. Paul Stevens), *Loving Justice* (12 studies by Bob and Carol Hunter).

GUIDES FOR SPECIFIC TYPES OF GROUPS

If you have a group that is serving a particular demographic, here are some specific ideas. Also note the list of studies for seekers on the back cover.

Women's Groups: *Women of the New Testament, Women of the Old Testament, Woman of God, Women & Identity, Motherhood*

Marriage and Parenting: *Marriage, Parenting, Grandparenting*